To Learn Is to Do

A Tikkun Olam Roadmap

Sharon D. Halper

Illustrations by Ann D. Koffsky

Library of Congress Cataloging-in-Publication Data

Halper, Sharon D., 1944-
To learn is to do: a tikkun olam roadmap / Sharon Halper; illustrated by Ann D.
Koffsky.
    p. cm.
    Summary: Presents lessons from the Torah, suggests ways of performing everyday acts
of caring, and lists organizations that help those in need.
    ISBN 0-8074-0729-1
    1. Ethics, Jewish—Juvenile literature. 2. Conduct of life—Juvenile literature. 3. Jewish
way of life—Juvenile literature. 4. Bible. O.T. Pentateuch—Commentaries—Juvenile literature. 5. Jewish religious education—Textbooks for children. [1. Ethics, Jewish. 2.
Conduct of life. 3. Judaism—Customs and practices.] I. Koffsky, Ann D., ill.
    BJ1285 .H35 2000
    296.3'6—dc21   00-036376

UAHC Press
New York

This book is printed on acid-free paper.

Manufactured in the United States of America

10 9 8 7 6 5 4 3

CONTENTS

A NOTE TO THE TEACHER

Many *tikkun olam* organizations are mentioned in this book. These organizations were chosen by the author because they exemplify different ways in which individual people try to do *tikkun olam*, using a variety of methods and resources. Some of these organizations are large and stable and have been around for a long time. Others are small, new, and without many resources. Some of these organizations will last; some will not. It is possible that by the time you use this book, some of these organizations will have folded, merged, or changed.

The inclusion of these organizations in this book is not an endorsement by the UAHC, but rather an invitation to learn about the wide range of *tikkun olam* being undertaken. What is important about these organizations is that they offer different models of hands-on *tikkun olam*. Feel free to substitute other organizations or models with which you may be more familiar or that have emerged since this book was published.

INTRODUCTION

A roadmap helps you to get from one place to another. It helps you to see how one road leads to others and shows you choices you have along your way. Living a Jewish life is like being on a road. It's full of choices and connections that lead to places you might not have expected.

For Jews, Torah is the main road. It shows us where we came from as a people and points each of us to new destinations. Studying Torah helps us to see that we can each follow different routes on our way and each have a wonderful, exciting trip.

For Jews, *tikkun olam*, the repair of our world, is the main task. The Jewish mystics taught that before the world was created, there was only God and that God's presence was everywhere. In order to make room for the creation of the world, God had to store some of the divine light. Somehow, in a mystical cosmic accident, the vessels storing God's light broke, and bits of this light were scattered everywhere on earth. Each time that we perform a mitzvah, a commandment, we find a spark of God in our world and help fix the world just a little bit.

This book is a *tikkun olam* roadmap, a tool to help you find sparks of God's light. It can help you to take a journey that will help to heal the world. There are so many possible roads on this journey that it will take your whole life! Each time you find a new road, a new entrance, a new possibility, your trip will become richer and the world will be just a bit better because of your travels through it.

No one takes this journey alone. Jews are travelers on long and crowded roads. Generations of Jews have come before us, and there are many Jews on this same journey with us now. Those who have come before us have built some of the stops we will visit on our way. The organizations and projects you will learn about, begun by Jews and nonJews alike, are all ways that people have built their journey. Each of them invites you to stop by and participate. Each offers you a way to carry our ancient texts with you on your trip through Jewish life.

You'll see that the road of Jewish living and world-healing has lots of "on-ramps" for you to try and loads of intersections that point to different possibilities of learning and doing. Along the way, you'll learn some of the language of the road—Hebrew, of course. You'll learn some of the language of Jewish world repair and see how we use it even in very everyday activities. And you'll learn how to drive your own personal world rescue vehicle.

Our trip will begin in our Jewish birthplace, learning about who we are and why this lifelong journey is part of our particular Jewish itinerary. Every trip requires an energy source. Our energy comes from Torah, which fuels us with very powerful ideas about who we are, as a people and as individuals. We are taught that we were created in the image of God, bound to God by a special pact or covenant, part of a holy people and designed to do acts of righteousness. Every time we use some of that energy, we are refueled to travel further. It's going to be a long and rewarding trip. Let's get going!

1 B'reishit
We Are Created in the Image of God

צֶלֶם אֱלֹהִים • *Tzelem Elohim*

In the Torah

In the beginning, the world is empty. God creates day and night, water and land, plants, stars, sun, moon, and animals. Then God creates people. They are created with a unique plan in mind.

GENESIS 1 | 27) And God created people in God's image, in the image of God people were created; male and female God created them. 28) God blessed them and said to them: "Be fertile and increase, fill the earth and master it...."

LOOKING AT THE TEXT

The Rabbis taught that the Torah doesn't use words unnecessarily.
Each word is there for a reason.
Why, then, does verse 27 mention people being created in God's image not once, but twice?

God's love for people is shown in two ways. One is creating them in God's image. But even greater is that God let us know that we are created in God's image.

— **PIRKEI AVOT**

Respecting Differences

Sometimes it is hard to remember that we are all created in God's image and therefore must treat each other with respect. Can you recall a time when you had a hard time remembering this?

How does it feel to be created in God's own image?

_____

What does this idea teach us about how to treat other people?

_____

Discover some important facts about the creation of men and women in this Creation story.

They were both created _____ **and at the same** _____ .

They were created with the responsibility of _____ .

Judaism has blessings for foods, for special events, for happy times and sad. There is even a blessing to be said when we see a person created differently from ourselves.

בָּרוּךְ אַתָּה יְיָ אֱלֹהֵינוּ מֶלֶךְ הָעוֹלָם, מְשַׁנֶּה הַבְּרִיּוֹת.

Baruch Atah Adonai, Eloheinu Melech ha-olam, m'shaneh habriyot.

BLESSED ARE YOU, ADONAI OUR GOD, RULER OF THE WORLD, WHO MAKES PEOPLE OF ALL TYPES.

Blessings shine a spotlight on the things we do and help us to see the world in a new light.

Think back to a time when you saw someone unusual. How did you feel?

_____

Would you have felt differently if you had said this blessing? How? Why?

_____

Doing Means Lending a Hand

BE A BLESSING

Many people face incredible challenges every day, and others help them meet those challenges. There are medications and treatments that cause people's hair to fall out. Locks of Love is an organization that collects human hair (at least eight inches long) from people who are cutting their hair so that people who have lost theirs can have human hair wigs. Having a fine hairpiece is one way to help restore their confidence and dignity.

What skill or blessing can you share in order to help someone else?

SAVING LIVES

The Rabbis taught: "And if one saves a single person, it is as if he saves the whole world."

MISHNAH

Explain this lesson in your own words.

_____

Suggest one way that we can remember this important lesson.

_____

God created life. We can help save lives in many ways.

Sometimes a smile, a helping hand, or a kind word helps to save someone's dignity or self-esteem. This is one form of saving a life.

Have you performed the mitzvah of *pikuach nefesh*, saving a life, recently?

What did you do? _____

THE UNIQUENESS OF CREATION

Everyone should know that since Creation no other person was created exactly the same. Every person is expected to perfect his or her unique qualities.

BAAL SHEM TOV

What is one of your unique qualities? _____

What can you do to perfect it? _____

Key Word: אֵל

Worksheet: Names of God

We refer to God by many names. What does each different name teach us about our ideas of God? What can each name teach you about yourself, created in the image of God?

The Lord our God יְיָ אֱלֹהֵינוּ

What does this name of God teach us...

about God? *Hes our leader.*

about ourselves? *We are what he is!*

When are we like lords? How can we do it in a godly way? *when were the oldst and or wiesest.*

God Almighty אֵל שַׁדַּי

What does this name of God teach us...

about God? *he is and/or was our creator*

about ourselves? *That we can also be creators*

When are we mighty? How can we be mighty in a godly way? *by being Assertive*

Master of the universe רִבּוֹנוֹ שֶׁל עוֹלָם

What does this name of God teach us...

about God? *that his name means to be master*

about ourselves? *we could be masters*

What do we master? How can we be masters in a godly way? *being a kind and consitorit master*

God Most High אֵל עֶלְיוֹן

What does this name of God teach us...

about God? *Hes nign in the sky*

about ourselves? *we are lower then him*

How can we raise ourselves up? How can we raise ourselves up in a godly way?

_____

Think of one way that you have been god-like today.

2 Noach
We Are Part of an Eternal Covenant

בְּרִית עוֹלָם • *B'rit Olam*

In the Torah

God grows angry at the lawlessness and violence of the people of the earth. God concludes that the way to cure the evils of the world is simply to save the only righteous man, Noah, and his family and to destroy the rest of humanity. So God floods the world. At the conclusion of the flood, life is ready to begin again.

GENESIS 9

8) And God said to Noah and his sons, 9) "I now create a covenant with you and your children yet to be born, 10) and with every living thing that is with you—birds, cattle, wild beasts—every thing that has come out of the ark, every living creature on earth. 11) I will keep My agreement with you:... never again will there be a flood to destroy the earth." 12) God further said, "This is the sign for the covenant between Me and you, and every living creature with you, for all ages to come. 13) I have set My bow in the clouds and it will be a sign of the covenant between Me and the earth."

LOOKING AT THE TEXT

In verse 9, God tells Noah that this promise, this covenant, would take place between Noah and his children and Noah's children not yet born.
Why would God have made this promise in this way?
How could a covenant be made with people who weren't born yet?
In verse 13, what is meant by the "bow in the clouds"?

Being God's Partner

In Hebrew, a covenant isn't "made," it's "cut."

Can you think of a covenant with God that is literally a "cut"?_____

_____

Can you think of an English expression that might come from this Hebrew usage?

_____

A "covenant" is a pact, a promise, between at least two partners.
In this covenant, God's promise to the world is very clear.
Our part of the promise is not spelled out clearly.

As God's partners in preserving the earth, what do you think we have to do to keep our side of the covenant?

_____

בָּרוּךְ אַתָּה יְיָ אֱלֹהֵינוּ מֶלֶךְ הָעוֹלָם,
זוֹכֵר הַבְּרִית וְנֶאֱמָן בִּבְרִיתוֹ וְקַיָּם בְּמַאֲמָרוֹ.
WE PRAISE YOU, ADONAI OUR GOD, RULER OF THE UNIVERSE,
YOU REMEMBER YOUR COVENANT WITH THE CREATION.

This is the blessing we say when seeing a rainbow. The blessing is a result of an event in our lives, but it draws us back to what biblical events?

> **All that we see... the heavens, the earth, and all that fills it...**
> **All these are the external garments of God.**
> **THE TANYA**

We can learn a lot about a person by looking at their clothes.
If everything on earth is God's "external garments" as this verse teaches us, what can we learn about God from looking at God's "clothes"?

BELIEVING IS DOING

Keeping our side of the covenant with God is to put what we believe into action. In some Jewish communities, a tree is planted when a new baby is born. A cedar is planted for the birth of a boy; a pine for a girl. When the child is married, some of the wood from the tree might be used for the chupah (the wedding canopy). Some have adapted this custom by planting trees in Israel in honor of a new baby.
Why is planting a tree particularly an appropriate way to honor the birth of a new baby?

Doing Means Taking Care

CARING FOR GOD'S CREATION

Trees add oxygen to the environment, bring beauty and shade to our lives, and produce wood that we use in numberless ways. The Jewish National Fund is an organization that plants and cares for trees and forests in Israel.

TAKING CARE OF THE EARTH

COEJL, the Coalition for the Environment and Jewish Life, is an organization that helps teach us the importance of taking care of the earth.

Think of your favorite Jewish holiday. What, if any, connection does it have to nature and the earth? What is one way that you can make caring for the earth part of the celebration?

Be a partner in the בְּרִית עוֹלָם, the eternal covenant, by being a guardian of the earth.

Take a walk around your house and think of changes in the way your family lives that you could make to help preserve the earth. Can you think of items in the supermarket or mall that you might not buy because of the impact they have on the earth?

It is forbidden to destroy anything that can be useful to people.

SHULCHAN ARUCH

This verse might be one of the earliest texts on recycling!

In what ways does recycling preserve the earth?

TAKING CARE OF PEOPLE

America's Second Harvest, the nation's largest domestic hunger relief organization, receives mainly surplus food from the nation's food and grocery industry and distributes it to food banks that serve needy people.

Do people who have a simchah at your synagogue know where to donate leftover food?

What can you do to help create a food bank in your synagogue?

Key Word: בְּרִית

Worksheet: Keeping the Covenant

The word בְּרִית, "covenant," is one we often find in Jewish life.

בְּרִית מִילָה is the covenant of circumcision, the ceremony that enters a baby boy into the Jewish people.

See Genesis 17:9–11 to see how that בְּרִית was created.

What is God's side of that covenant? _____

בְּנֵי בְּרִית, "sons of the covenant," is also known as B'nai B'rith, a Jewish *tzedakah* organization.

Find out if anyone you know is a member of B'nai B'rith.

Find out what the group does in your area.

אוֹת בְּרִית is a token or sign of a covenant, like the rainbow.

We see signs of an important personal covenant all the time.
Hint: Think of married people. Many of them wear an item that was given to them as an *ot b'rit*, a sign of the covenant they made with their partner.

What is it? _____

בְּרִית עוֹלָם, "everlasting covenant," is used in the Shabbat *Kiddush*.

What is one thing you can do this week as a sign of the "everlasting covenant" of

Shabbat? _____

3 K'doshim
We Are a Holy People

גּוֹי קָדוֹשׁ • *Goy Kadosh*

In the Torah

The Book of Leviticus is often called the Law of the Levites, the Priests. But it is also a blueprint for holy living for all Israelites. In a portion called "the Holiness Code," we are taught what it means to live a life of holiness.

LEVITICUS 19 | 1) Adonai spoke to Moses, saying: 2) Speak to all the Israelites and tell them: You shall be holy, for I, Adonai your God, am holy.

LOOKING AT THE TEXT

This short section says something very powerful about people.

Explain, in your own words, what it says. _____

_____

_____

Living a Life of Holiness!

HOW HOLINESS HAPPENS

The following commandments come from "the Holiness Code" in Leviticus 19. They are rules for holy living.

LEVITICUS 19 | 9) When you harvest your land, do not harvest all the way to the edges of your field... 10) leave them for the poor and the stranger...

What it Intends: _____

_____

How we can make it happen: _____

_____

LEVITICUS 19 | 14) Do not insult the deaf, or place a stumbling block before the blind.

What it Intends: _____

_____

How we can make it happen: _____

_____

LEVITICUS 19 | 15) Do not judge unfairly: do not favor the poor or show honor to the rich.

What it Intends: _____

_____

How we can make it happen: _____

_____

WE BRING HOLINESS THROUGH BLESSINGS

The words אֲשֶׁר קִדְּשָׁנוּ, *asher kid'shanu*, that begin many blessings remind us that we are commanded to perform holy acts and that we are grateful to God for the chance to do so.

Think of all the blessings that contain the words אֲשֶׁר קִדְּשָׁנוּ, *asher kid'shanu*, and list them:

בָּרוּךְ אַתָּה יְיָ אֱלֹהֵינוּ מֶלֶךְ הָעוֹלָם
אֲשֶׁר קִדְּשָׁנוּ בְּמִצְוֹתָיו וְצִוָּנוּ...

Baruch Atah Adonai, Eloheinu Melech haolam,

asher kid'shanu b'mitzvotav v'tzivanu....

Blessed are You, Adonai, Creator of the universe,

You make us holy with Your commandments and command us to...

Surprise!

There is no blessing to be recited before performing the mitzvah of *tzedakah*.

Why do you think this is the case? In the space below, write one in English.

Baruch Atah Adonai, Eloheinu Melech haolam, asher kid'shanu...

Blessed are You, Adonai, Creator of the universe, You make us holy with Your commandments and command us to...

_____

_____

WORLD BEING REPAIRED

Doing Means Performing Acts of Holiness

JUDAISM IS A "HOLINESS HUNT"...
A SEARCH FOR WAYS TO MAKE THE ORDINARY SPECIAL

By our words, our actions, and our prayers, we try to add holiness to our everyday lives.

In your own words, define holiness.

קִדּוּשִׁין, *kiddushin,* is the Hebrew word for marriage. The word teaches us that marriage is holy, a special relationship.

קִדּוּשׁ, *Kiddush,* is the blessing we recite before drinking wine or grape juice. We are reminded that God's gifts are holy; they are blessings.

קַדִּישׁ, *Kaddish,* is the name of the prayer we recite in memory of those we have loved. Our prayer reminds us that God's name and our memories are holy, sacred.

Jews are commanded to "be holy." One way we do that is to bring a feeling of the extra-ordinary into the ordinary. It takes practice to see the world as full of extraordinary things. Think about something in your everyday life, and explain how it is holy, special. Can you do it with an alarm clock? homework? your bad-tasting medicine?

IMPROVING LIVES WITH ACTS OF HOLINESS

In Jewish tradition, working is considered a sacred task. We are taught to treat those who work for us with dignity. Often that ideal is not followed. Caridad Asensio has devoted her life to bringing dignity to the workers who pick the fruits and vegetables we all enjoy. Often these workers who travel from place to place to pick crops have no medical care, and their children receive only a poor education. Caridad brings קְדֻשָׁה into their lives by helping these workers, caring for their children, and treating them with dignity.

BRINGING HOLINESS TO THE END OF A LIFE

A חֶבְרָה קַדִּישָׁא (*chevrah kaddishah*), "holy society," is a community organization that prepares the deceased for burial. The חֶבְרָה קַדִּישָׁא performs the last mitzvah that anyone can for another person. Other organizations provide free burial for those whose families are unable to afford a dignified funeral. There are free burial societies in many communities. One such society is the Hebrew Free Burial Society of Greater Washington.

Key Root: ק־ד־שׁ

Worksheet: Practice Holiness!

For each word:

- Highlight the root קדשׁ.
- Read each word CAREFULLY!
- Try to identify each "holiness" word. Where have you heard each one?

קִדּוּשִׁין _____

קָדוֹשׁ _____

קַדִּישׁ _____

וְיִתְקַדַּשׁ _____

נַקְדִישׁ _____

קִדְּשָׁה _____

קִדְּשָׁנוּ _____

"HOLINESS" PHRASES IN JEWISH LIFE

אַתְּ מְקֻדֶּשֶׁת לִי   **What makes a relationship holy?** _____

"YOU ARE CONSECRATED
[MADE HOLY] TO ME" (FROM   _____
THE MARRIAGE CEREMONY)
_____

אֲרוֹן הַקֹּדֶשׁ   **What makes a cabinet holy?** _____

THE HOLY ARK (THE   _____
TORAH'S "HOME")
_____

לְשׁוֹן הַקֹּדֶשׁ   **How can a language (or our tongues) be holy?** _____

"HOLY TONGUE" (THE   _____
HEBREW LANGUAGE)
_____

Sh'mot
We Pursue Righteousness

צֶדֶק • *Tzedek*

In the Torah

A new Pharaoh, one who does not know Joseph, comes to power in Egypt. Pharaoh is afraid of the Israelites because there are so many of them. He thinks they might one day join with his enemies to fight against him. Even though he tries to make their lives difficult by enslaving them, they continue to increase. This makes Pharaoh even angrier, and he tries to limit their numbers in other ways.

EXODUS 1

15) The king of Egypt spoke to the Hebrew midwives, Shifra and Puah, 16) saying, "When you deliver the Hebrew women... if it is a boy, kill him; if it is a girl, let her live." 17) The midwives, fearing God, did not obey the king; they let the boys live. 18) So the king of Egypt called for the midwives and said to them, "Why are you letting the boys live?" 19) The midwives answered Pharaoh, "... Before the midwife can come to the Hebrew women, they have already given birth." 20) So God was good to the midwives; and the people grew. 21) And because the midwives feared God, God granted them families.

LOOKING AT THE TEXT

In this text, we never learn the name of the Pharaoh, the powerful king of Egypt. But we do know the names of the midwives. What does this tell us about the difference between Pharoah and the midwives?

In a place where people are without courage, act bravely.

— **PIRKEI AVOT**

It is very hard to do the right thing when people around you are not.
Can you think of a time when you have been in that situation? What did you do?

Understanding Righteousness

כִּי יְדַעְתִּיו לְמַעַן אֲשֶׁר יְצַוֶּה אֶת־בָּנָיו וְאֶת־בֵּיתוֹ
אַחֲרָיו וְשָׁמְרוּ דֶּרֶךְ יְהֹוָה לַעֲשׂוֹת צְדָקָה וּמִשְׁפָּט לְמַעַן
הָבִיא יְהֹוָה עַל־אַבְרָהָם אֵת אֲשֶׁר דִּבֶּר עָלָיו:

I have singled him out, that he may teach his children and those to come to keep the way of the Lord and do what is righteous and correct.

GENESIS 18:19

In this verse, God gives one reason why the Jewish people were created and what is our job in the world. Find the word "righteous" in the Hebrew text and circle it.

TZEDAKAH OR CHARITY?

Tzedakah is usually translated as "charity." The word "charity" comes from the Latin root that means "love." According to that definition, a person gives charity because they are a loving person or because they love the person who is in need.

Tzedakah is not about love. It's about what we have to do because we are Jews. Remember the line from Genesis 18:19? We were created to do righteous acts in this world. *Tzedakah* is part of our job as Jews. Charity is optional. *Tzedakah* is not. Does understanding what *tzedakah* really means change what you think about why and how Jews give *tzedakah*?

Justice, justice shall you pursue.

צֶדֶק צֶדֶק תִּרְדֹּף

DEUTERONOMY 16:20

List three ways you can "pursue justice" this week.

1. _____   2. _____

3. _____

THE *TZEDAKAH* CHALLENGE

Is it *tzedakah*, or is it charity? Fill in the blanks with the correct choice.

1. Based on a person's love for others: _____

2. Based on one's *b'rit* (covenant) with God: _____

3. A choice you might make: _____

4. You have to do it! _____

Doing Means Helping

HELP THE RIGHTEOUS

During the terrible years of the Holocaust, there were gentiles (non-Jews) who risked their own lives to rescue Jews. Often they did not even know the people they helped. As they age, many of these righteous rescuers now need our help. The Jewish Foundation for the Righteous was created in order to help them. Find out more about the foundation. One way to help these righteous gentiles is to "twin" with one of them when you become bar or bat mitzvah.

HONOR THE RIGHTEOUS

One way we honor people is by learning about them and ensuring that their righteousness is not forgotten. Yad Vashem, the Holocaust memorial in Jerusalem, plants trees in honor of the righteous gentiles, which line the beautiful Avenue of the Righteous. Varian Fry is the only American who was honored as one of the "Righteous among the Nations" by Yad Vashem. He saved hundreds of Jewish artists and writers who were stranded in Marseilles, France, as the Germans advanced. Others rescuers whose stories will fascinate you are Oscar Schindler, Chiune Sugihara, the people of Le Chambon (France), Raoul Wallenberg, King Christian X, and the people of Denmark. Look for materials in your synagogue or school library, or on the Internet.

REMEMBER AND CARE FOR THE RIGHTEOUS

The righteous of our own people who suffered simply because they were Jewish and who survived the Holocaust need to be remembered and cared for. The Blue Card is an organization that provides financial support to Holocaust survivors. Blue Card helps them to live the rest of their lives with dignity.

Key Root: צ־ד־ק

Worksheet: *Tzadik/Tzadeket*

TO BE A *TZADIK/TZADEKET*

In Hebrew, someone who is considered righteous is called a *tzadik* צַדִּיק (for a man) or a *tzadeket* צַדֶּקֶת (for a woman). To be called a *tzadik* or *tzadeket* is one of the greatest honors possible.

A RIGHTEOUS PERSON

In your opinion, what makes someone a righteous person?
List three things that make someone qualify for the description of "righteous."

1. _____

2. _____

3. _____

Do you know anyone you would call a *tzadik* צַדִּיק or *tzadeket* צַדֶּקֶת? What did the person do to earn that title?

Becoming a *tzadik/ tzadeket* is not easy. It takes practice.
We are given many chances to show that we can learn what it means to be righteous.
Think of a time when you were given an opportunity to be righteous.
Being righteous isn't about being perfect. It's about making good choices in difficult situations. Sometimes we only realize later that we should have made a better choice. Hopefully that will help us the next time we have a choice to make. You may have made a righteous choice, or maybe you did not. Either way, you learned something.

Describe your experience below.

The circumstances:

_____

The choices you had:

_____

What choices you made:

_____

Is there anything you would do differently next time?

_____

5 *Vayigash*
We Perform Acts of Caring

חֶסֶד • *Chesed*

In the Torah

Joseph starts out as a slave in Egypt and becomes an important and influential aide to Pharaoh. There is a famine in Canaan, where Joseph's family lives, and his brothers go to Egypt in the hope of finding food. They come before Joseph but do not recognize him. But he knows who they are, and after some time he reveals himself to them. He assures them that he is not angry that they sold him into slavery and caused him to go down to Egypt.

GENESIS 45

5) Do not be upset that you caused me to be here; it was in order to save lives that God sent me here ahead of you.... 7) God sent me ahead so that I could ensure your survival.... 11) I will provide for you—for there are still five years of famine ahead—so that you and all of your household may not suffer from want of food.

LOOKING AT THE TEXT

Joseph's answer shows that he knows the ultimate source of our food.

What is that source? _____

Caring for the Hungry

A full bag is heavy, but an empty one is heavier.

————— PROVERBS

We all know that a full bag is harder to carry than an empty one!

So what is this proverb trying to teach? _____

Advice and words will not fill an empty belly.

————— MISHLE YEHOSHUA

According to this text, when you see a hungry person, what should you do first?

_____

Do you agree? Why or why not? _____

Where there is no bread, there is no Torah.

————— PIRKEI AVOT

Why do you think the Rabbis felt that in order to have Torah, you need to have bread?

Do you agree? Why or why not? _____

Can you think of an example of a time in Jewish history when there was more Torah

than bread? _____

PERFORM ACTS OF *CHESED* WHEREVER YOU GO!

Caring for the hungry is one way you can show your chesed.

CARING AT SCHOOL

How can you help your school care for the hungry? _____

What happens to the "small change" that students have left from their lunch money?

_____

What happens to food that is left over and can't be re-served? _____

_____

CARING AT YOUR SYNAGOGUE

How can you help your synagogue care for the hungry? _____

_____

Are leftovers from temple events donated to a local soup kitchen? _____

_____

Do families of b'nei mitzvah receive the phone number of a local soup kitchen before

their simchahs? _____

CARING AT HOME

How can you help your family care for the hungry? _____

_____

What does your family do with the money from bottle returns? _____

_____

Can you donate the money you save with coupons? _____

_____

Doing Means Feeding

FEEDING AND WELCOMING THE HUNGRY

Students at the Hebrew Union College–Jewish Institute of Religion, the school that teaches people to be rabbis, cantors, and educators, run a weekly soup kitchen in New York City. Every Monday they set tables with flowers, cook a nourishing meal, and even prepare buttons and thread to do repairs on guest's clothing. What can we learn from the way the students perform this mitzvah?

Rabbi Tanchuma, though he needed only one portion of meat for himself, would buy two; one bunch of vegetables, he would buy two—one for the poor and one for himself.

KOHELET RABBAH

How can you be like Rabbi Tanchuma? _____

_____

_____

RESCUING FOOD

The Potato People "rescue" fresh fruits and vegetables that have not been sold from farms and food distributors and deliver them to organizations that feed hungry people. Without them, this edible food would go into the trash. If you want to be a "food rescuer," find out what the stores in your area do with food that can no longer be sold. You might be able to organize parents to pick up and deliver usable food.

Key Root: ח־ס־ד

Worksheet: God Cares about Us

The *siddur* reminds us constantly that God cares about us. Since we are created in God's image, it is our job to be like God and also perform acts of caring.

Practice these *siddur* phrases about ח־ס־ד:

בְּרֹב חַסְדֶּךָ	abundant lovingkindness
גְמִילוּת חֲסָדִים	acts of lovingkindness
גּוֹמֵל חֲסָדִים טוֹבִים	bestower of lovingkindness
חַסְדֵי אָבוֹת	the caring of our ancestors
חֵן וָחֶסֶד וְרַחֲמִים	grace and love and mercy
וְאַהֲבַת חֶסֶד	to love kindness
לְעוֹלָם חַסְדוֹ	everlasting caring

Circle the three root letters in each of the phrases above.

What is an act of חֶסֶד that you've done lately? _____

_____

Yitro
We Give Honor

כָּבוֹד • *Kavod*

In the Torah

The Israelites are freed from Egyptian slavery and spend three months in the Sinai Desert. While the people hear thunder and see lightning, Moses goes up to the top of the mountain and receives the Ten Commandments. The first four commandments deal with how we treat God. The fifth is about a very important relationship—the relationship with our parents.

EXODUS 20 | 12) Honor your father and mother, so that you may live a long time in the land that Adonai is giving you.

LOOKING AT THE TEXT

"Honor" is a difficult word to understand.

In your own words, explain what you think it means to honor someone.

Honoring Our Parents

. . . .

Rabbi Shimon bar Yochai said, "The most difficult of all mitzvot is 'Honor your father and mother.'" (*Tanchuma*)

What do you think he meant by that? _____

_____

What makes it difficult to honor someone, even someone you love? _____

_____

Search out how God expects you to treat your parents. What acts do you think God

wants you to do? _____

HONORING THE TORAH

In many congregations, whenever the Ten Commandments are read, the congregation rises to hear them. Standing is a way of showing כָּבוֹד, respect, and a way of showing that we remember that our ancestors stood at Mount Sinai.

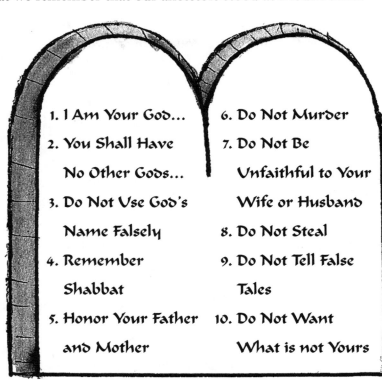

1. I Am Your God...
2. You Shall Have No Other Gods...
3. Do Not Use God's Name Falsely
4. Remember Shabbat
5. Honor Your Father and Mother
6. Do Not Murder
7. Do Not Be Unfaithful to Your Wife or Husband
8. Do Not Steal
9. Do Not Tell False Tales
10. Do Not Want What is not Yours

PAIRS OF COMMANDMENTS

Some people think of the commandments as pairs. For example, the first is paired with the sixth, the second is paired with the seventh, and so on. Each commandment has a relationship with its "partner." How do you think the Fifth Commandment is related to the Tenth Commandment?

Doing Means Honoring

HONORING THE ELDERLY

> Myriam's Dream is an all-volunteer organization that supports dozens of projects all over the world that help the elderly. They establish workshops for the elderly that provide them with meaningful work like binding books or knitting. This work gives the elderly a sense of dignity, purpose, and community. Myriam's Dream honors the parents of our communities! Find out how you can be a part of their projects.

HONORING DREAMS

> We can honor people by honoring their dreams. Second Wind Dreams is an organization that helps honor the dreams of people who live in nursing homes by making those dreams come true. Imagine an elderly person who dreams of riding in a helicopter or a motorcycle! You can help make someone's dream come true.

HONORING OUR PARENTS

Rabbi Shlomo Riskin has written that the promise of "long life" in return for honoring our parents doesn't necessarily mean that the person who obeys will live many years.

Rather, he says that by obeying our own parents, we are linked to all the parents who have come before us.

Therefore, we are given "long life" by being connected to all the generations in the long chain of Judaism.

Keeping Your Link Strong

You are an important link in your family's chain. Label one link: your ancestors; the next: your grandparents; the next: your parents; the last: YOU.

How do you keep your link strong? What have you received from your ancestors that you will "link" to the future?

Key Word: כָּבוֹד

Worksheet: Showing Honor

With a little planning, we can show כָּבוֹד in everything we do.
How can we show כָּבוֹד for ourselves and others in the following places?

AT HOME _____

IN THE CLASSROOM _____

IN THE SCHOOL LUNCHROOM _____

ON THE PLAYGROUND _____

IN SYNAGOGUE _____

In Hebrew, refreshments offered to a guest are called כָּבוֹד. How is כָּבוֹד different from just a snack?

_____

_____

What are things that Jews do in honor of the Sabbath, לִכְבוֹד שַׁבָּת? What is something you would like to try לִכְבוֹד שַׁבָּת?

_____

_____

7 *Lech L'cha*
We Can Be a Blessing

בְּרָכָה • *B'rachah*

In the Torah

The story of our people begins in chapter 12 of Genesis, with God's call to Abraham. Abraham answers God by setting forth as God has commanded him to do. This is the start of Jewish history.

GENESIS 12 | 1) Adonai said to Abram, "Go forth from the land in which you were born and from your father's house to the land that I will show you. 2) And I will make of you a great nation, / And I will bless you; / I will make your name great , /And you will be a blessing. / 3)… And all the families of the earth / Shall bless themselves by you."

LOOKING AT THE TEXT

In verse 1, God tells Abram to leave his land and his father's house. Leaving his land would obviously mean leaving his father's house. Why the repetition?

Saying Blessings

Rashi, an eleventh century commentator born in France, believed that until the events of chapter 12 of Genesis, only God had the ability to perform blessings. God had blessed Adam and Noah, but now Abraham was given the privilege to bless anyone he chose.

Rashi's interpretation reminds us that we can be like God in many ways.
Like God, we can bring blessing to people. How have you been a blessing to someone?
This is the text in which Abraham, and all his ancestors, are chosen by God.

According to the text, what were Jews chosen to do? _____

_____

100 BLESSINGS A DAY

Blessings help change everyday events into special moments. Traditionally Jews are supposed to say 100 blessings each day. Blessings are a way to say "Thank You, God," or "Please God," or "God, You make us special," or "Wow! Good going, God."

The Blessings Challenge

Can you imagine saying 100 blessings? Try saying 100 blessings this week. It's not as hard as you might think. You can create your own blessings.
Can you think of a blessing for brothers and sisters? for homework? for the alarm clock?

_____

_____

_____

_____

_____

_____

Keep a blessings diary on this page by listing the blessings you said in each category.

בָּרוּךְ אַתָּה יְיָ אֱלֹהֵינוּ מֶלֶךְ הָעוֹלָם

Baruch Atah Adonai, Eloheinu Melech haolam...

THANK YOU...

בָּרוּךְ אַתָּה יְיָ אֱלֹהֵינוּ מֶלֶךְ הָעוֹלָם

Baruch Atah Adonai, Eloheinu Melech ha-olam,

PLEASE...

בָּרוּךְ אַתָּה יְיָ אֱלֹהֵינוּ מֶלֶךְ הָעוֹלָם

Baruch Atah Adonai, Eloheinu Melech ha-olam...

YOU MAKE US SPECIAL BY COMMANDING US TO...

בָּרוּךְ אַתָּה יְיָ אֱלֹהֵינוּ מֶלֶךְ הָעוֹלָם

Baruch Atah Adonai, Eloheinu Melech ha-olam...

WOW!...

Doing Means Being a Blessing

BE A BLESSING...

Blessings help us to see the world in new ways. They remind us that our lives are filled with amazing things and that our job is to bring blessings to others.

... BY TURNING GARBAGE INTO BLESSINGS TO BE SHARED

Jewish life is about sharing our blessings. The Redistribution Center is an organization that reminds us not to forget all the ways that we are blessed. It was begun by Ranya Kelly when she found 500 pairs of shoes in a dumpster behind her local mall. It was easier for the store to throw the unsold shoes away than to give them to people who needed them. Today this organization redistributes millions of dollars worth of merchandise that would otherwise wind up in garbage dumps or landfills. They work with some of America's largest companies to bring blessings to people who need the clothing, shoes, blankets, and other items that stores no longer wish to sell.

... BY TURNING TRASH INTO THE BLESSINGS OF FOOD

Syd Mandelbaum started Rock and Wrap It Up! in 1994. Rock and Wrap It Up! was started in order to rescue food from rock concerts that would have otherwise been thrown away. More than 130 bands have helped donate 1.8 million pounds of food to 5 million hungry people! Now other industries do the same thing, making certain that their leftover food gets to people who need it. Students in middle school through college have begun similar programs in their own schools.

Think of three ways you could bring blessings to people who live in your own community.

1. _____

2. _____

3. _____

Key Root: ב־ר־ךְ

Worksheet: We Have Lots of Blessings...

AND BLESSING WORDS

All of the following words have something to do with blessing. Circle the root ב־ר־ךְ as it appears in each word. Practice reading each word.

בָּרוּךְ	blessed, praised
הַמְבוֹרָךְ	whom we praise
בְּרָכָה	blessing
בְּרָכוֹת	blessings
בָּרְכוּ	the "Call to Worship"
בֶּרֶךְ	knee

TO READ AND REMEMBER

Each of the following is used to say "welcome" in Hebrew. Each literally means "Blessed is the one(s) who is/are coming."

Practice reading them, and try to use them correctly!

Masculine singular	בָּרוּךְ הַבָּא!
Masculine plural	בְּרוּכִים הַבָּאִים!
Feminine singular	בְּרוּכָה הֲבָאָה!
Feminine plural	בְּרוּכוֹת הַבָּאוֹת!

These Hebrew greetings contain a word that "welcome" just doesn't have! What is that extra word?

_____

T'tzaveh
We Keep the Light Burning

נֵר תָּמִיד • *Ner Tamid*

In the Torah

The Israelites construct the *mishkan*, the portable sanctuary that they will carry in the desert. They will use this *mishkan* to worship God. In these lines, God gives Moses the instructions regarding the light that is to shine there.

EXODUS 27 | 20) You shall teach the Israelites to bring you clear olive oil for lighting, for lighting lamps regularly. 21) Aaron and his sons [the priests] shall set them up in the Tent of Meeting, outside the curtain which is in front of the Tablets of the Law, to burn from evening to morning before Adonai. This shall be done as a responsibility by the Israelites for all time, throughout the ages.

LOOKING AT THE TEXT

Keeping the light burning seems to be the job of the priests, but they couldn't do it alone. Who has the responsibility to make sure that the light could burn?

Lighting Up the World

> **Every Jew must light the *ner tamid* (eternal light) in his own heart, and not only in the synagogue and school. He must light it in all activities when he deals with other people.**
>
> **PARDES YOSEF**

The eternal light is not just a light for the sanctuary! There is a light that we can carry with us everywhere. How do you show people that your personal eternal light is burning?

BEING A LIGHT

Who "needs" the light?

A Midrash says that God doesn't need the light, but God wanted to show us that God needs people.

Seeing the eternal light reminds us that only people can keep God's light burning in our world.

How do you help to keep the light of God burning bright in the world?

_____

> **I created you, and appointed you a covenant people, a light to the nations**
>
> **ISAIAH 42:6**

Speaking for God, the prophet Isaiah reminds us that the Jewish people are commanded to be a light for other peoples to see. What does Isaiah mean by being "a light"? When have you been "a light" for others?

Think of two ways that the Jewish people can be a light to the nations.

1. _____

2. _____

Doing Means Being a Light

Try to picture the eternal light in your sanctuary. Is it electric?

Is it a real candle? If so, who changes the candle, and how often? _____

_____

LIGHT UP THE WORLD

Ziv means "radiance." The ZIV Tzedakah Fund helps support the work of "mitzvah heroes," people who light up dark corners of this world. One of those people is Janet Marchese. She arranges for children with Down Syndrome, a form of mental retardation, to be adopted by families who will love and care for them. Find out about the fund and some of their other "mitzvah heroes" by getting a copy of the ZIV Annual Report.

For a mitzvah is a light.

PROVERBS

This line from Proverbs teaches us that when we perform mitzvot, we add light to the world.

Explain in your own words what this line is trying to say. _____

_____

How many mitzvah lights have you lit this week?_____

_____

LET THE LIGHT SHINE ONCE AGAIN

The Eldridge Street Synagogue, on the Lower East Side of New York City, was built in 1887. When Jews moved out of the neighborhood, the once magnificent synagogue was left to deteriorate. Today the building gleams once again with the efforts of people who have donated time and money to bring it back to life. Is there an old synagogue in your area that could use help to "shine" proudly once again?

Key Word: אוֹר

Worksheet: Lights in Jewish Life

Light, אוֹר, plays an important role in several Torah sections. One of those times is when the lights of the world are first turned on.

וַיֹּאמֶר אֱלֹהִים יְהִי אוֹר וַיְהִי־אוֹר

God said, "Let there be light"; and there was light.

GENESIS 1:3

Then God makes two kinds of lights—a "big one" that shines during the day and a "small one" for the night.

the big light – הַמָּאוֹר הַגָּדֹל

the small light – הַמָּאוֹר הַקָּטֹן

The following are names of special Jewish lights. Read and identify when they are used:

נֵרוֹת **candles**

נֵר שֶׁל יוֹם טוֹב **holiday lights**

נֵר שֶׁל שַׁבָּת **Shabbat lights**

נֵר שֶׁל חֲנֻכָּה **Chanukah lights**

Jews light candles for many reasons, some happy and some sad.
List two other kinds of "Jewish lights" and what they are used for.

1. _____

2. _____

9 Sh'mini
We Eat What Is "Fit"

כָּשֵׁר • *Kasher*

In the Torah

The Book of Leviticus contains the laws for the Levites, who were the priests in the Temple in Jerusalem. These lines from Leviticus are laws that help us bring holiness into every area of our own lives, in particular the laws of kashrut. These laws concern what we may eat, or what food is kosher.

 **LEVITICUS 11**

2) These are the land creatures you may eat... : 3) any animal that has true hoofs, with clefts through the hoofs, and that chews its cud.... 9) These you may eat of the things that live in water: anything in water that has fins and scales.

LOOKING AT THE TEXT

The requirements for a kosher animal are:

1. _____

2. _____

The requirements for a kosher fish are:

1. _____

2. _____

Eating With Care

WHY KOSHER?

The Torah tells us "Which?" foods are kosher. Many people have also asked "Why?" we have these laws.

Levi Isaac of Berdichev, an eighteenth century rabbi, taught that the laws of kashrut were **not** about food, but rather they were about our mouths and how we use them. He taught that if we were careful about what we put **into** our mouths, then we'd also be careful about what comes **out** of our mouths. In other words, following the laws of kashrut would remind us to stay away from evil speech.

Maimonides, the great commentator and physician, taught that the foods that were forbidden were unhealthy and that the laws of kashrut were based on medical reasons.

Many disagreed with him, saying that if that were true, then Torah would be nothing more than a medical book. A cure for food-related sickness would make the Torah, and the laws in the Torah, unnecessary.

Mordecai Kaplan, a twentieth-century rabbi, taught that having to keep kosher had helped save the Jewish people by reminding them that they are a special people.

A MENU OF BLESSINGS: DIFFERENT BLESSINGS FOR DIFFERENT FOODS

Being aware of what we eat also reminds us to think about **how** we eat. Keeping kosher, eating what is "fit," reminds us that there is also a "fit" attitude toward eating. This attitude includes being grateful for all that we have. Blessings are one way we show that we are grateful.

בָּרוּךְ אַתָּה יְיָ אֱלֹהֵינוּ מֶלֶךְ הָעוֹלָם

BLESSED ARE YOU, ADONAI OUR GOD, SOVEREIGN OF THE UNIVERSE,

The blessing said when eating...

... bread:

הַמּוֹצִיא לֶחֶם מִן הָאָרֶץ

WHO BRINGS FORTH BREAD FROM THE EARTH.

... cakes and pastry:

בּוֹרֵא מִינֵי מְזוֹנוֹת

CREATOR OF ALL MANNER OF THINGS.

... fruits that grow on trees:

בּוֹרֵא פְּרִי הָעֵץ

CREATOR OF THE FRUIT OF THE TREES.

... fruits that grow in the earth:

בּוֹרֵא פְּרִי הָאֲדָמָה

CREATOR OF THE FRUIT OF THE EARTH.

... liquids other than wine and foods other than those "covered" by the other blessings.

שֶׁהַכֹּל נִהְיֶה בִּדְבָרוֹ

BY WHOSE WORD ALL THINGS COME INTO BEING.

Doing Means Eating Jewishly

THE SOURCE OF FOOD

The *Motzi*, the blessing before eating bread, refers to God, the One who brings forth bread from the earth.
Try saying the blessing before your next meal.
Does saying the blessing help you to remember something? What?

בָּרוּךְ אַתָּה יְיָ אֱלֹהֵינוּ מֶלֶךְ הָעוֹלָם

BLESSED ARE YOU, ADONAI OUR GOD, SOVEREIGN OF THE UNIVERSE,

הַמּוֹצִיא לֶחֶם מִן הָאָרֶץ

WHO BRINGS FORTH BREAD FROM THE EARTH.

All creatures eat.
Jews make the act of eating holy by reciting blessings before and after eating.

BEING THANKFUL FOR FOOD

> **When you have eaten your fill, and have built fine houses to live in, and your herds and flocks have multiplied, and your silver and gold have increased, and everything that you own has done well, Be careful that your heart does not grow haughty and you forget Adonai your God.**
>
> **DEUTERONOMY 8:12–14**
> **[part of *BIRKAT HAMAZON*]**

Birkat HaMazon, the blessing said after eating, is commanded in the Torah.

Based on these verses, what danger was "the *Birkat*" intended to avoid?

FOOD FOR A HOLY PURPOSE

Kibbutz Yahel, a Reform kibbutz in Israel, raises pomelos. Pomelos are sweet citrus fruits that look like extra-large grapefruits. The kibbutz "rents" their pomelo trees to individuals and groups. The money raised from the "rental" of the tree supports a summer camp that brings poor Arab children from Tel Aviv to enjoy a vacation in the desert. This program really combines food and holiness!

Key Word: כָּשֵׁר

Worksheet: *Kashrut* Debate

Veal, the meat of a calf, can't be considered "fit to eat" even though it is kosher, because the animals are confined to cages so tiny that they can't move around.

Agree or disagree? Explain why.

_____

_____

Fruits and vegetables, although kosher, are not "fit to eat" if they are overpackaged in plastic bags and trays that will remain in landfills long after the food is gone.

Agree or disagree? Explain why.

_____

_____

כַּשְׁרוּת *KASHRUT* = "HOLINESS IN EATING"

It isn't just being fresh or cooked properly that makes food fit to be eaten.

The laws of *kashrut* כַּשְׁרוּת are written in the Torah. These laws were explained and interpreted by later generations of Jews.

Here are modern interpretations of the laws of kashrut. These new interpretations not only look at what God said in the Torah, but ask how what we eat affects the world.

Next to each opinion, mark whether you agree or disagree, and explain why.

Foods that are raised or harvested by underpaid migrant farm workers can't be "fit to eat" because the needs of the people who grow the food aren't considered.

Agree or disagree? Explain why.

_____

_____

Foods that are sprayed with chemicals that are potentially dangerous to the earth or the health of people can't be considered "fit to eat."

Agree or disagree? Explain why.

_____

_____

What else might we consider when we choose what is "fit" to eat?

_____

Think of two things you can do to bring a new attitude—one that is כָּשֵׁר—to your eating.

1. _____

2. _____

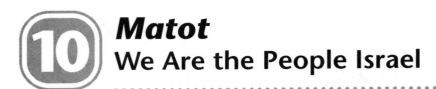

Matot
We Are the People Israel

עַם יִשְׂרָאֵל • *Am Yisrael*

In the Torah

In these verses, the years of wandering in the desert are finally coming to an end, and the Promised Land is about to be settled. The people have lived as members of tribes since they were freed from slavery in Egypt, so the question of where each tribe will settle must be answered. Two of the tribe are the Reubenites and the Gadites.

NUMBERS 32

1) The Reubenites and the Gadites owned many cattle. They noticed that land [east of the Jordan River] was a region suitable for cattle, 2) and the Gadites and the Reubenites came to Moses... and the leaders of the community, and said... 5) "It would be a favor to us if this area were given to us; do not move us across the Jordan." 6) Moses replied to the Gadites and the Reubenites, "Are your brothers going to war while you stay here?"... 16) They answered him by saying, "Here we will build places for our flocks and towns for our children."

LOOKING AT THE TEXT

The Rabbis criticized the Gadites and the Reubenites for their response in these verses.

Why do you think they did so?

Do you think they did anything wrong here? Why or why not?

Being Part of a Community

Some people were sitting in a ship when one of them took a drill and started to drill a hole under his seat. The other passengers asked him what he was doing. He said to them, "What has this to do with you? Am I not boring a hole under my own seat?" They answered, "But the water will come in and drown us all."

— **VAYIKRA RABBAH**

Imagine that the Gadites, the Reubenites, and Moses had been the people in that boat.
Who would have been drilling the hole?
Who would have warned that everyone would drown because of the hole?

Rabbi Hillel summarized the problem of balancing our responsibilities in the following way:

If I am not for myself, who will be for me? But, if I am only for myself, what am I? And, if not now, when?

— **PIRKEI AVOT**

List three things that you do for yourself.

1. _____

2. _____

3. _____

List three things that you do for others.

1. _____

2. _____

3. _____

Do not separate yourself from the community.

— **PIRKEI AVOT**

PART OF A COMMUNITY

Jews can't be Jewish alone! We need a community within which we can be Jewish.
Think of Jewish history and life and of the events that go on in your synagogue.
Then list five ways that show that Jews live within a community.

1. _____

2. _____

3. _____

4. _____

5. _____

Doing Means Celebrating

ANYONE CAN HAVE A "TWIN"!

We usually think of twins as being two siblings who were born at the same time. But being a twin can also be a way to care about someone else and to share with that person.

The following Jewish organizations ask that you share your bar/bat mitzvah celebration with people all over the world, so that your personal *simchah* becomes a reason for others to celebrate! But you don't have to be thirteen to be a twin. Consider sharing the joy of your birthday by making a donation to one of these groups.

North American Conference on Ethiopian Jewry: Become a "twin" with an Ethiopian child now living in Israel and provide the money for a special field trip or even a set of books for an entire class.

MAZON—a Jewish Response to Hunger: Become a "twin" to some of the hungry of the world by sharing the blessings of your *simchah*.

World Union for Progressive Jewry: Become a "twin" with children who have never had to chance to learn about Judaism through the Reform movement's program for children in the former Soviet Union.

The ZIV Tzedakah Fund: Become a "twin" with a person whose *tzedakah* work you admire from the ZIV Tzedakah Fund Annual Report, and make a donation to share your joy with the people they help.

The Jewish Foundation for the Righteous: Become a "twin" with a righteous person who helped Jews during the Holocaust, and learn more about righteousness and caring.

PERSONAL CELEBRATIONS AS OPPORTUNITIES FOR CARING FOR OTHERS

Think of another way to share your personal celebration with others.
Design a birthday party, a Thanksgiving dinner, or a Chanukah celebration that includes doing *tikkun olam*. Write an idea below.

Key Word: יִשְׂרָאֵל

Worksheet: An Israel Word List

The word "Israel" can mean either the land or the people. There are many important Jewish expressions that use this word.

Here are some that are useful to know:

בְּנֵי יִשְׂרָאֵל	Children of Israel	No matter how old a Jew is, we are all בְּנֵי יִשְׂרָאֵל.
שְׁמַע יִשְׂרָאֵל	Hear O Israel!	The start of our most important prayer.
מְדִינַת יִשְׂרָאֵל	the State of Israel	The modern nation of Israel, "born" in 1948.
אֶרֶץ יִשְׂרָאֵל	the Land of Israel	This was first promised to Abraham over 3,000 years ago.
יִשְׂרְאֵלִי	an Israeli man or boy	
יִשְׂרְאֵלִית	an Israeli woman or girl	

Complete each sentence with the proper Israel word(s). (Some words are repeated!)

All of _____recite _____.

_____ have always prayed to have a homeland in _____

_____.

One day you might visit _____ and meet a _____

_____ or a _____ with whom you might speak Hebrew.

Emor
We Celebrate Being Jewish

שִׂמְחָה • *Simchah*

In the Torah

The Book of Leviticus contains laws for the priests as well as laws for the members of the Holy People—all of us!

LEARN FROM THE TEXT!

Below you will find the Torah verses that mention some of the major holidays. What can you learn about the holidays from the text?

LEVITICUS 23

4) These are Adonai's set times, the sacred occasions, which you will celebrate each at its chosen time. 5) In the first month, on the fourteenth day of the month, at twilight, there will be a passover offering to Adonai, 6) and on the fifteenth day of that month, Adonai's Feast of Unleavened Bread. You will eat unleavened bread for seven days.

What holiday is this? _____

Look at a Jewish calendar. What is the name of the month? _____

_____

What will you eat? _____ **For how long?** _____

Counting from the Feast of Unleavened Bread, how many days until the next holiday?

_____

According to the Torah, what does this holiday celebrate? _____

_____

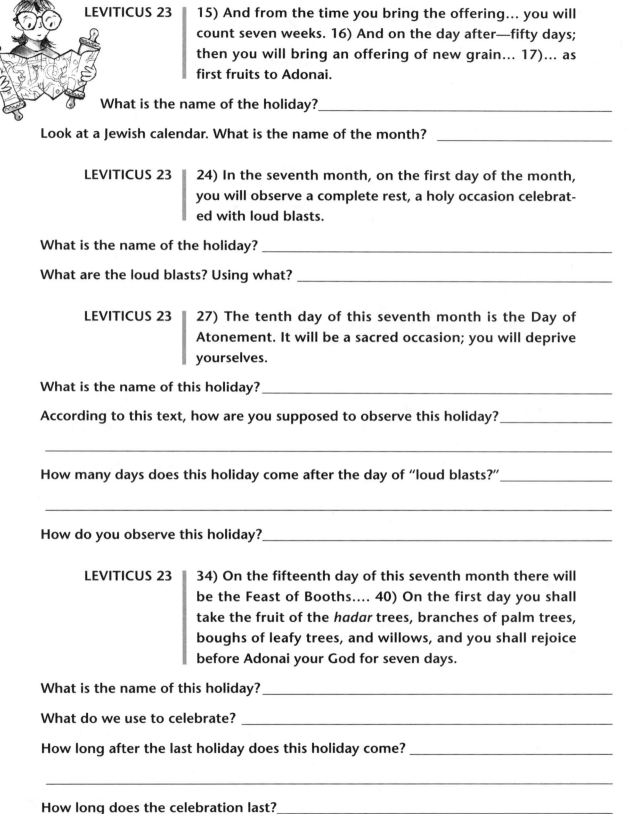

LEVITICUS 23 | 15) And from the time you bring the offering… you will count seven weeks. 16) And on the day after—fifty days; then you will bring an offering of new grain… 17)… as first fruits to Adonai.

What is the name of the holiday?_____

Look at a Jewish calendar. What is the name of the month? _____

LEVITICUS 23 | 24) In the seventh month, on the first day of the month, you will observe a complete rest, a holy occasion celebrated with loud blasts.

What is the name of the holiday? _____

What are the loud blasts? Using what? _____

LEVITICUS 23 | 27) The tenth day of this seventh month is the Day of Atonement. It will be a sacred occasion; you will deprive yourselves.

What is the name of this holiday? _____

According to this text, how are you supposed to observe this holiday?_____

_____

How many days does this holiday come after the day of "loud blasts?"_____

_____

How do you observe this holiday?_____

LEVITICUS 23 | 34) On the fifteenth day of this seventh month there will be the Feast of Booths…. 40) On the first day you shall take the fruit of the *hadar* trees, branches of palm trees, boughs of leafy trees, and willows, and you shall rejoice before Adonai your God for seven days.

What is the name of this holiday?_____

What do we use to celebrate? _____

How long after the last holiday does this holiday come? _____

_____

How long does the celebration last?_____

Celebrating the Holidays

WHAT WE SAY, PRAY, THINK, AND FEEL...

Passover

> **In every generation, each Jew is to feel as though he/she went out of Egypt.**
>
> **THE PASSOVER HAGGADAH**

The Haggadah adds to the Torah text by telling us how we are to observe the Feast of Unleavened Bread.

How did you feel when you went out of Egypt? _____

Shavuot

On Shavuot our ancestors brought the best of their crops as sacrifices to God. This helped them feel closer to God. Today on Shavuot, in many synagogues we celebrate receiving the Torah by celebrating with our oldest students as they observe their Confirmation. Whenever we do what we believe God wants of us, we too feel closer to God.

When do you feel close to God?

_____

_____

_____

Sukkot

> **You will live in booths seven days... in order that future generations will know that I made the Israelites live in booths when I brought them out of Egypt.**
>
> **LEVITICUS 23:42–43**

How do you think it felt to live in booths? How does it make you feel when you remember that our ancient Jewish family lived in booths?

_____

Rosh HaShanah

> **Today is the birthday of the world.**
>
> **HIGH HOLY DAY MACHZOR**

At any birthday, including the world's, we make wishes for the one celebrating the birthday.

Make your own wish for the world. _____

Yom Kippur

> **This shall be to you a law for all time: to make atonement for the Israelites for all their sins once a year.**
>
> **LEVITICUS 16:34**

To atone means to ask for forgiveness. To atone for something we have done to another person, we must ask that person for forgiveness. To make it meaningful, we must try hard never to commit that act again. Whenever we atone, we help fix the world.

For what do you think you need to atone? _____

Doing Means Healing

· ·

... WHAT WE DO! WE HEAL THE WORLD AS WE CELEBRATE!

Passover

When I remember that I was a slave in Egypt, it reminds me to _____

This is how I can do it: _____

Shavuot

I believe that God wants people to _____

This is how I will do it: _____

Sukkot

Because my ancient Jewish family lived in

booths, that reminds me to _____

I will _____

Rosh HaShanah

This is one way I will help make my wish for the world come true: _____

Yom Kippur

One thing I will do to improve my relationship with _____ is _____

HEALING WITH PROM DRESSES AND BAR MITZVAH SUITS

The Glass Slipper Project, an organization begun in Chicago by two young lawyers, is a clearinghouse for prom dresses and other accessories. The group collects gently used dresses and lends them to girls who cannot afford to buy their own. Other groups do the same with bar mitzvah suits and bat mitzvah dresses in day schools and synagogues.

HEALING WITH WEDDING DRESSES AND BOWLS OF SOUP

The Rabbanit Bracha Kapach does all she can to help people who need help. She packs Passover food packages, runs a summer camp, cooks Shabbat meals for the needy, and provides wedding dresses for needy brides. Tourists visiting Israel often stop at her home to deliver a wedding dress that they have brought with them.

Key Root: שׁ־מ־ח

Worksheet: Our Celebrations

WE ARE LUCKY TO HAVE MANY REASONS FOR CELEBRATIONS AND MANY WORDS OF CELEBRATION!

Practice reading these celebratory words:

שָׂמֵחַ	joyful
שִׂמְחָה	a happy occasion
שְׂמָחוֹת	more than one happy occasion
שִׂמְחַת תּוֹרָה	celebration of the Torah
חַג שָׂמֵחַ	Happy Holiday!
שִׂמְחָה וְשָׂשׂוֹן	happiness and joy
שִׂמְחַת בַּת	celebration of the birth of a daughter
זְמַן שִׂמְחָתֵנוּ	the Time of Our Rejoicing (another name for *Sukkot*)

Fill in the correct celebration word(s):

A greeting: _____

Fall Festivals: _____

A lifecycle event: _____

When you go to a wedding, you are attending _____.

If you are going to a bar mitzvah in the morning and attending a wedding at night,

your day will be full of _____.

12 *Mishpatim*
We Love the Stranger

וַאֲהַבְתֶּם אֶת הַגֵּר • *Veahavtem et Hager*

In the Torah

The Torah contains as many as 613 mitzvot, or commandments. These mitzvot deal with every part of our lives—how we worship and celebrate, how we live and love, how we treat one another. This passage is an example of one mitzvah.

EXODUS 22 | 20) You shall not wrong a stranger or oppress him, for you were strangers in the land of Egypt.

LOOKING AT THE TEXT

This mitzvah commands us to behave in a certain way.

What is the reason that we have to behave ethically toward the stranger who lives among us?

Remembering that We Were Strangers

BEING A STRANGER

Being a "stranger" can mean lots of different things. We usually think of a stranger as a person who is new to a place, but there are other ways that a person might be a "stranger." Sometimes just being different can make someone feel like a stranger.
Think of one reason someone might feel like a stranger.

_____

LOVE THE STRANGER

The Torah reminds us not once, not twice, but thirty six times to befriend or love the stranger. What does this repetition tell you about about how simple or difficult it is to carry out this mitzvah? Why do we need to be reminded so much?

_____

> **You shall not wrong a stranger, for you know the feelings of a stranger, because you were strangers in the land of Egypt.**
>
> **EXODUS 23:9**

Have you ever felt like a stranger? Why? _____

What does it feel like to be a stranger? _____

> **You also must befriend the stranger, for you were strangers in the land of Egypt.**
>
> **DEUTERONOMY 10:19**

To "befriend" someone does not mean that you have to be "best friends."

Explain one way that you can do as this verse from Torah commands. _____

_____

... YOU WERE STRANGERS IN THE LAND OF EGYPT

[Adonai] befriends the stranger, providing him with food and clothing.

DEUTERONOMY 10:18

What is this verse reminding us to think about when we give *tzedakah* or perform

other mitzvot? _____

You shall not abuse a needy or poor laborer, whether a fellow countryman or a stranger in your land.

DEUTERONOMY 24:14

Explain, in your own words, what this verse is commanding us to do.

_____

Do you think this commandment is still necessary today?

_____

Doing Means Loving

HOW CAN WE "LOVE THE STRANGER"?

Remember what it was like to be a stranger in the land of Egypt

Complete the following sentences.

Because I was a stranger in the land of Egypt...

I remember that _____

I won't ever _____

I will try _____

I think it is important to _____

Someday I would like to be able to _____

BEING NEW CAN MAKE SOMEONE FEEL LIKE A STRANGER

Loving the Stranger by Welcoming New Immigrants
The Hebrew Immigrant Aid Society, HIAS, was founded in 1880 by a group of Jewish immigrants who escaped from persecution in Europe. Since then, HIAS has assisted more than four and a half million people! They help new immigrants with everything from completing paper work and taking the exam to become a citizen, to finding lost relatives, to awarding scholarships so that new immigrants can make a good life in their new home.

BEING DIFFERENT CAN MAKE SOMEONE FEEL LIKE A STRANGER

Loving the Stranger by Helping People
One day a child came to the school office because his feet hurt. It turned out that his feet hurt because his shoes were too small and his parents didn't have the money to buy new shoes. Elodie Silva heard about this child and started an organization, Shoes That Fit, to provide children with basics like clothes and shoes. That way, no child will have to feel embarrassed about being different, and no child will have to walk in shoes that don't fit.

Key Root: א־ה־ב

Worksheet: You Shall Love

When we pray, we are acknowledging God's love. When we love, we are acting in a Godly way. Here are some expressions that show how we meet God through love.

LOVE IN THE TORAH...

Love your neighbor as yourself.	וְאָהַבְתָּ לְרֵעֲךָ כָּמוֹךָ

LEVITICUS 19:18

LOVE IN THE SIDDUR...

Find these prayers in your *siddur*:

אַהֲבָה רַבָּה   "Deep is Your love"   On page _____ of our prayer book.

אַהֲבַת עוֹלָם   "Unending is Your love"   On page _____ of our prayer book.

וְאָהַבְתָּ   "You shall love"   On page _____ of our prayer book.

LOVE IN JEWISH LIFE...

אוֹהֵב שָׁלוֹם   a lover of peace

אַהֲבַת תּוֹרָה   love of Torah

אַהֲבַת לִמּוּד   love of learning

אַהֲבַת יִשְׂרָאֵל   love of the Jewish people

אַהֲבַת אֶרֶץ יִשְׂרָאֵל   love of the Land of Israel

Select one of these "loves" in Jewish life and explain how something you do demonstrates that kind of love.

GLOSSARY OF SOURCES

Baal Shem Tov
(1700–1760)—Israel ben Eliezer, founder of the Chasidic movement. Also known as the Besht.

Hillel
(1st century B.C.E.)—A rabbinic Sage who founded the school known as Bet Hillel.

Kohelet Rabbah
A collection of **midrashim** on Ecclesiastes.

Machzor
High Holy Day prayer book.

Midrash
(Hebrew for "searching out")—The name given to biblical commentaries in which the text is explained in ways other than the literal meaning. Midrashim help to bring modern meaning from the biblical text.

Midrash Hagadol
A collection of rabbinic interpretations by David ben Amram Adani, a Yemenite scholar of the first and second centuries.

Mishnah
Part of the **Talmud** edited by Judah HaNasi.

Pirkei Avot
(lit. "Ethics of the Fathers")—A tractate of the **Mishnah** containing ethical teachings of the Rabbis from the third century b.c.e. to the third century C.E.

Proverbs
A biblical book, part of the Writings, which consists mainly of moral sayings.

Shimon bar Yochai
(2nd century C.E.)—Said to have been the author of the *Zohar*, a mystical interpretation of Torah.

Shulchan Aruch
The Prepared Table, the code of Jewish law written by Joseph Caro, a sixteenth century Spaniard.

Talmud
(Hebrew for "teaching")—Consists of the Mishnah and the Gemara, collected records of academic discussions compiled from the second to the fifth centuries C.E.

Tanchuma
A collection of midrashim said to have been collected by Rabbi Tanchuma in the fourth century C.E.

Tanya
A work by Shneur Zalman of Lyady (1747–1813), which attempted to explain Chasidic teaching.

Vayikra Rabbah
An early collection of rabbinic **midrashim** on Leviticus.

LIST OF *TIKKUN OLAM* ORGANIZATIONS

Chapter 1. We Are Created in the Image of God

Locks of Love
1640 South Congress Avenue, Suite 104
Palm Springs, FL 33461
(888) 896-1588
(561) 963-1677
www.locksoflove.com

Chapter 2. We Are Part of an Eternal Covenant

Jewish National Fund
42 East 69th Street
New York, NY 10021
(800) 542-TREE
(212) 879-9300
www.jnf.org

COEJL, The Coalition for the Environment and Jewish Life
443 Park Avenue South
New York, NY 10016
(212) 684-6950, ext. 210
www.coejl.org

America's Second Harvest
116 South Michigan Avenue, Suite 4
Chicago, IL 60603
(800) 532-FOOD
(312) 263-2303
www.secondharvest.org

Chapter 3. We Are a Holy People

Hebrew Free Burial Society of Greater Washington
c/o Kamerow, Weintraub & Swain
11400 Rockville Pike
Rockville, MD 20852
(301) 468-2424

Caridad Asenio
Migrant Association of South Florida
at the Caridad Health Campus
8645 West Boynton Beach Boulevard
Boynton Beach, FL 33437
(561) 737-6336

Chapter 4. We Pursue Righteousness

The Jewish Foundation for the Righteous
305 Seventh Avenue, 19th floor
New York, NY 10001
(212) 727-9955
www.jfr.org

The Blue Card
1 West 34th Street, #404
New York, NY 10001
(212) 239-2251
bluecard@erols.com
www.bluecard.org

Chapter 5. We Perform Acts of Caring

Soup Kitchen
Hebrew Union College-Jewish Institute of Religion
1 West Fourth Street
New York, NY 10012
(212) 674-5300

Potato Project
Society of Saint Andrew
3383 Sweet Hollow Road
Big Island, VA 24526
(800) 333-4597
(804) 299-5956
www.endhunger.org

Chapter 6. We Give Honor

Myriam's Dream, Inc.
Linda Kantor, President
52 Wellington Drive
Orange, CT 06477

Second Wind Dreams
4031 Willows Way
Marietta, GA 30062
(770) 977-3528
gatric@aol.com
www.secondwind.org

Chapter 7. We Can Be a Blessing

The Redistribution Center
7736 Hoyt Circle
Arvada, CO 80005
(303) 431-0904

Rock and Wrap It Up!
Syd Mandelbaum
405 Oceanpoint Avenue
Cedarhurst, NY 11516
(877) 691-FOOD
www.rockandwrapitup.org

Chapter 8. We Keep the Light Burning

ZIV Tzedakah Fund
Write to Naomi Eisenberger, 384 Wyoming
Avenue, Millburn, NJ 07041; or check out the
ZIV website at www.ziv.org.

Chapter 9. We Eat What Is Fit

Kibbutz Yahel's "Pomelos for Peace" program
ARZA/World Union, NA
633 Third Avenue
New York, NY 10017
(212) 650-4280, arzawupjna@uahc.org

Chapter 10. We Are the People Israel

North American Conference on Ethiopian Jewry
132 Nassau Street
New York, NY 10038
(212) 233-5200
NACOEJ@aol.com
www.circus.org/nacoej

MAZON—A Jewish Response to Hunger
12401 Wilshire Boulevard, Suite 303
Los Angeles, CA 90025-1015
(310) 442-0020
www.shamash.org/soc-action/mazon/

World Union for Progressive Jewry
UAHC
633 Third Avenue
New York, NY 10017
(212) 650-4090

(The ZIV Tzedakah Fund and the Jewish Foundation
for the Righteous, mentioned in other sections, also
have "twinning programs.")

Chapter 11. We Celebrate Being Jewish

Rachel Hart
The Glass Slipper Project
(312) 409-4139
www.glassslipperproject.org

The Rabbanit Bracha Kapach
12 Lod Street
Jerusalem, Israel
phone: 02-624-9296

Chapter 12. We Love the Stranger

Hebrew Immigrant Aid Society
333 Seventh Avenue
New York, NY 10001-5004
(212) 967-4100
www.HIAS.org

Elodie Silva
Shoes That Fit
112 Harvard #43
Claremont, CA 91711
(909) 482-0050,
www.shoesthatfit.org